Bravo! 2

Judy West

Course consultant
C.J. Moore

HEINEMANN

Hello again!

Lesson 1   What's she doing?

Listen

Come here, children. Press V for visit.

We're off to a school club.

Listen and match

Sally's   making a small kite.
Sue's   playing on the computer.
Jim's   making a big kite.
Tommy's   making a box.
Sarah's   writing a letter.

Look

What's he doing?
He's writing a letter.

What's she doing?
She's reading a book.

Ask and answer

 What's she doing?  She's posting a letter.

watch TV

make a kite

draw a square

read a letter

draw a circle

What are you doing?

Sing ♪

What's he doing?
He's washing his hands.
He's brushing his teeth.

What's she doing?
She's brushing her hair.
She's clapping her hands.

Lesson 2 It's working

Listen

1. Hello. What's the matter? — Electrobox isn't working.
2. Oh, dear.
3. What are you doing? — I'm mending Electrobox.
4. Now it's working again. Amazing! — Yes, it's working.
5. Thank you, Miss Electra. — Not at all, Pete. Bye, bye.

Point and say

What are you doing? — I'm running.

1. I'm riding my bike.
2. I'm eating a pizza.
3. I'm skipping.
4. I'm reading.

Look

It's working.   It isn't working.   She isn't reading.   She's reading.

Ask and answer

Is he reading?

No, he isn't reading. He's writing.

eating?   skipping?   writing?

Play a game

What am I doing?

What am I doing?

Are you eating a pizza?

Are you brushing your teeth?

Are you skipping?

Are you reading?

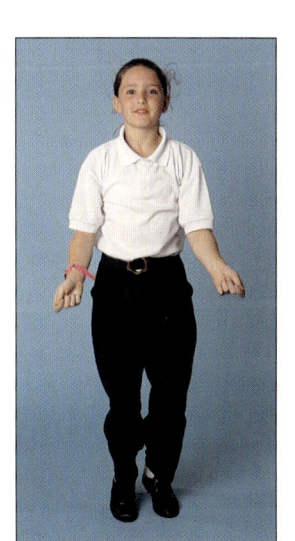 

seven 7

Lesson 3   Monday, Tuesday...

Listen 🔊   **Days of the week**

Listen and point 🔊

Point and say

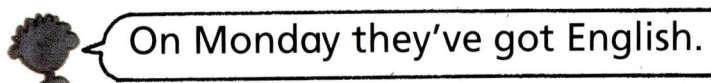
On Monday they've got English.

On Tuesday they've got...

Ask and answer

What have you got on Monday? — I've got English
What have you got on Tuesday? — I don't know

Monday	English
Tuesday	?
Wednesday	Maths
Thursday	Computers
Friday	French

What have you got on Wednesday?

Sing ♪

I'm riding in my time machine
I'm riding it right now
Monday, Tuesday, Wednesday,
Thursday Friday, Saturday, Sunday

Remember
Monday, Tuesday, Wednesday, Thursday } = one week
Friday, Saturday, Sunday

Lesson 4 It's half past...

Look

It's half past one.    It's half past four.

It's half past two.    It's half past seven.

Ask and answer

 What are Polly and Pete doing at half past eleven today?

They're catching the bus.

Visit to the Zoo

11.30 Catch bus
12.30 Have lunch
1.30   Visit zoo
4.30   Go home

Today!

English Club Monday

Tennis lessons

Remember
1 hour = 60 minutes

10 ten

Listen and decide

Listen for the feeding times.
Say **'Yes, that's right.'** or **'No, that's wrong.'**

They're feeding the crocodiles at three o'clock.
They're feeding the monkeys at half past three.
They're feeding the lions at half past two.
They're feeding the penguins at three o' clock.

What time are they feeding the lions?
What time are they feeding the penguins?

Play a game

Find these words in two minutes.

half	past
six	hour
seven	time
ten	one
two	
clock	
minute	

h	a	l	f	p	s	t
s	i	x	h	a	e	i
f	t	a	o	s	v	m
m	i	n	u	t	e	e
x	f	p	r	o	n	e
t	e	n	t	w	o	t
d	c	l	o	c	k	x

Lesson 5 Speak up! Three Five Ten

Listen and point

Three Friday Thank you Football Thirty
Table Five Ten Fifteen
Tennis Thursday Tuesday

Say

1. 30   2. 10   3. ⚽   4. 3   5. 🪑   6. 15

Sing ♪

Are you running, are you walking?
Are you listening, are you talking?
Are you reading or are you playing a game?

I'm not running, I'm not walking
I'm not listening, I'm not talking
I'm not reading, I'm not playing a game

I'm just singing a little song
A little song for you

Lesson 6 Revision 1

A Copy and complete

1. Have you got a hammer?
   No, ...
2. Has he got short hair?
   Yes, ...
3. Has he got a green nose?
   Yes, ...
4. Have you got a calculator?
   Yes, ...
5. .... bump on your head?
   Yes, ...
6. What's she doing?
   .... a book.
7. What's he doing?
   ....a kite.
8. What's she doing?
   .... her hair.
9. What are you doing?
   .... a pizza.
10. Is he reading?
    ....

B Say

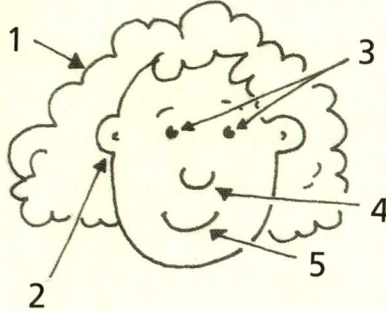

C Complete

Sunday ....
Wednesday ....
....

D Copy and complete

What's the time?

1  2  3

4  5

Now I can:
- use 'have got'.
- talk about faces.
- say 'What am I doing?'
- say the days of the week.
- tell the time.

Lesson 7   Can you...?

7

Look

Point and say

I can see a shirt. I can't see an egg.

a shirt
an egg
a shoe
an owl
a hat
a ball
a key
a clock
a parcel
a book
an apple
an orange

Ask each other

How many letters can you read?

fifteen 15

Lesson 8 — Can she...? Can he...?

Listen

1. Look. I can juggle. Can you juggle, Annie?

Yes, of course I can. Watch me. One, two, three ...

2. No, you can't!

It's that bee. Where's that bee?

3. Can you juggle and jump?

Yes, I can ...

4.

Point and match

Can Annie juggle?   No, she can't.
Can Bill juggle?   Yes, she can.
Can Bill juggle and jump?   Yes, they can.
Can Annie juggle and jump?   Yes, he can.
Can they juggle?   Yes, he can.

Ask and answer

Can she juggle?

Can he juggle?

Can you juggle?

16 sixteen

Look

Ask each other

Play a game

How many times can you ... ?

In one minute, how many times can you...

1 write your name?
2 count 1 - 10 ?
3 touch your toes?

Start now!

I can write my name ten times in one minute.

Lesson 9   next to   near   in front of

Listen

Come here please, children. Press V for visit.

We're off to a restaurant.

Listen and match

There are four people   chicken and chips.
We're eating   the drinks.
There are two people   lunch.
He's bringing   they're speaking French.
They're having   sitting at a table.
They aren't speaking English   sitting near the window.

Look

Hello.

Polly's sitting next to Pete.
She's near the door.
Pete's next to Polly.
Miss Electra's standing in front of the blackboard.
She's speaking English.

Ask each other

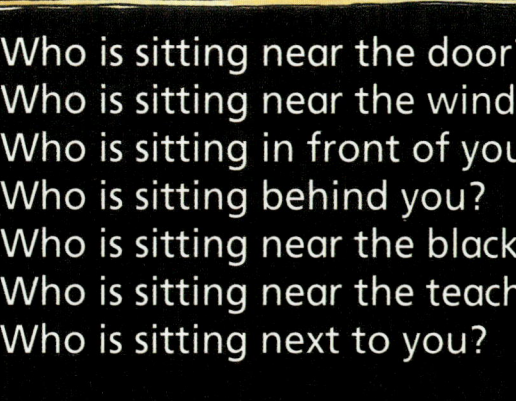

Who is sitting near the door?
Who is sitting near the window?
Who is sitting in front of you?
Who is sitting behind you?
Who is sitting near the blackboard?
Who is sitting near the teacher?
Who is sitting next to you?

Say

Hot chicken, hot chicken, hot chicken on Sunday
Cold chicken, cold chicken, cold chicken on Monday

Fish and chips, fish and chips, fish and chips on Tuesday
Egg and chips, egg and chips, egg and chips on Wednesday

Lesson 10 Let's... Yes, lets!

Listen

Ask and answer

Are they singing? — Yes, it is.
Are they dancing? — Yes, they are.
Is Polly singing? — No, she isn't.
Is Electrobox singing? — Yes, she is.
Is Miss Electra dancing? — No, they aren't.

20 twenty

Look

Let's sing. Let's run. Let's write. Let's read.

Point and say

Come on, let's skip. Yes, let's!

skip   play football   swim   skateboard

dance   juggle   watch TV   ride our bikes

Sing ♪

Electrobox is an amazing thing
Let's sing about Electrobox...

Electrobox is an amazing thing
Electrobox is an amazing thing
Electrobox is an amazing thing
It can talk and it can sing

I can talk and I can sing.

Electrobox is an amazing thing
Electrobox is an amazing thing
Electrobox is an amazing thing
It can read and it can spell

Lesson 11   January, February...

Listen

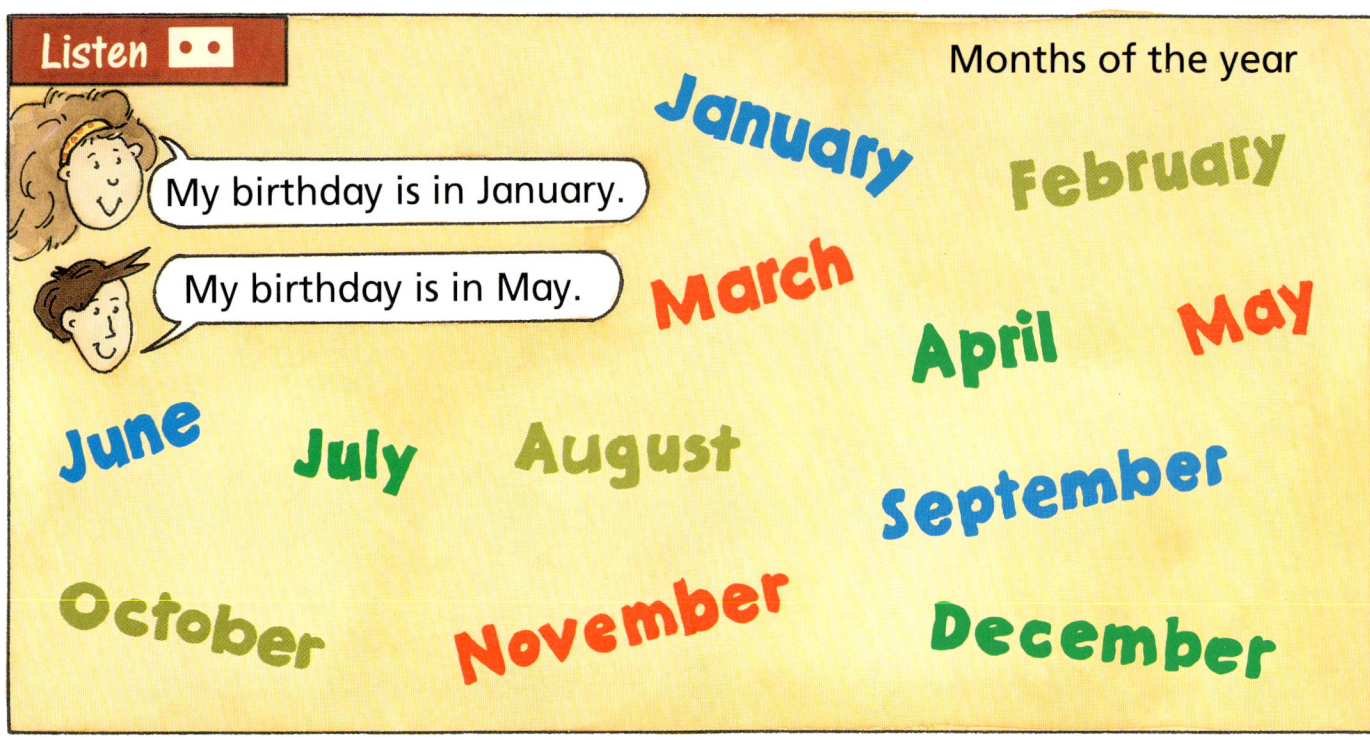

Months of the year

My birthday is in January.
My birthday is in May.

January, February, March, April, May, June, July, August, September, October, November, December

Point and say

Lucy's birthday is in March.

UUGSAT   ETSPEMEBR   PLAIR

UJEN   HACRM   EEEDCMBR

22 twenty-two

When's your birthday?

Ask each other

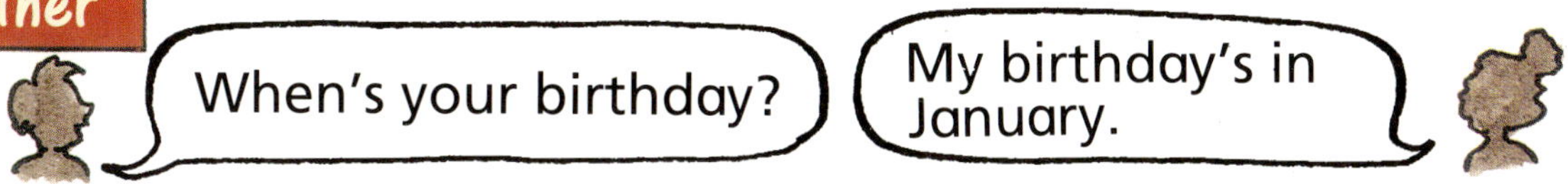

When's your birthday?

My birthday's in January.

Birthday Class Survey

January	✓								
February									
March									
April									
May									
June									
July									
August									
September									
October									
November									
December									

How many birthdays are there in August?

Play a game

How many days?

A How many days are there in June?

B Thirty.

Remember
In February there are 28 or 29 days.

Lesson 12   20 - 100

Listen

Say the numbers from head to tail.

Count in tens.
Count in twenties.

Ask and answer

What number is this? — It's thirty-two.

Listen and complete

Complete the see-saw sums.

$30 + 40 = 20 + 50$ $80 + \square = 90 + 10$ $60 + 15 = 100 - \square$

$20 + 15 = \square + 5$ $58 + \square = 42 + 18$ $70 - 8 = 12 + \square$

Read and decide

1 There are four weeks in one month.
How many weeks are there in five months?

2 There are twelve months in one year.
How many months are there in three years?

3 There are seven days in one week.
How many days are there in four weeks?

4 There are sixty minutes in one hour.
How many minutes are there in half an hour?

Number game

A What's my number?
B Twenty-three.
   What's my number?
A Thirty-four.
   My number and your number make fifty-seven.

twenty-five 25

Lesson 13 Speak up! hiss buzz

Listen and point

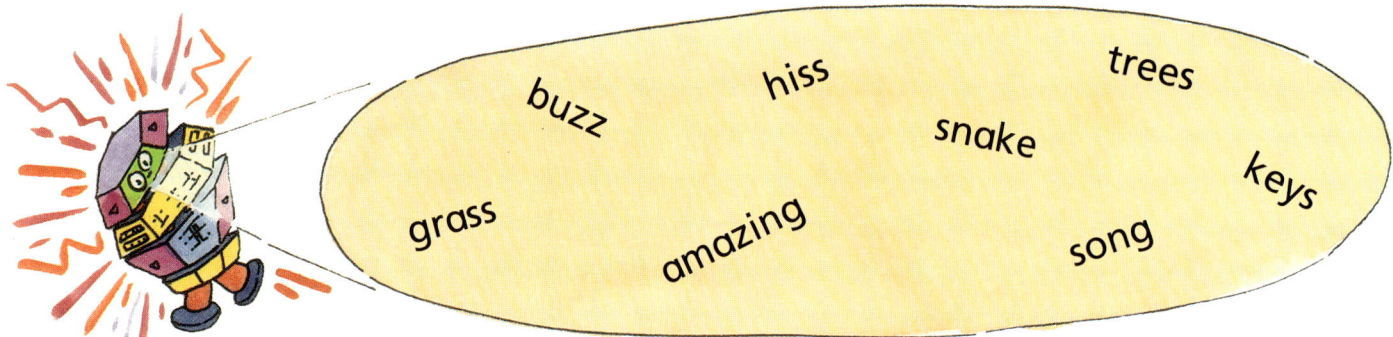

buzz hiss trees
snake
keys
grass amazing song

Say

1

2

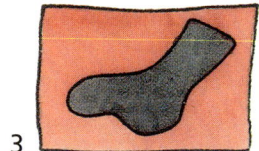
3

4

Sing ♪

Can you hear that funny buzz?
Can you hear that funny buzz?
Yes, I can
I can hear it in the trees
Buzz, buzz, buzz, buzz

Can you hear that funny hiss?
Can you hear that funny hiss?
Yes, I can
I can hear it in the grass
Hiss, hiss, hiss, hiss

Lesson 14 Revision 2

A Copy and complete

1 Let's sing.
   Yes, ...
2 ....
   Yes, let's!
3 .... is your birthday?
   It's .... January.
4 Can he juggle?
   ....
5 There are .... days in one week.
6 Can she swim?
   ....
7 Can he dance?
   ....
8 Can she run?
   ....

B Say

C Write in words

1 50   2 60   3 75

D Copy and complete

1 .... many .... in one hour?
   There are 60 minutes.
2 .... days .... in four weeks?
   There are 28 days.
3 How .... days .... June?
   There are thirty days.
4 .... see a bee?
   No, I can't.

E Copy and complete

January .... May
....
....

Now I can:
- use 'I can'.
- say 'Where's ...?'
- use 'Let's ...'
- say the months of the year.
- count to 100.

Lesson 15   Do you like...?   I like...

Listen

Look

Do you like bananas?
Yes, I do.

Do you like spaghetti and ice cream?
No, I don't.

Ask and answer

Do you like apples?
Yes, I do.
No, I don't.

apples
oranges
bananas
grapes
pears
peaches

Ask each other

Do you like ...?

Class survey

Yes, I do. = ✓   No, I don't. = ✗

						pizza						
						spaghetti						
						ice cream						
						ants						
						dogs						
						cats						
						football						
						basket ball						
						tennis						
						Maths						
						English						
					✓	French	✗					

I like...   I don't like...

twenty-nine 29

Lesson 16   Does...like...? He likes...   She likes...

Listen

Ask and answer

Does Annie like blue bananas?   No, he doesn't.
Does Andy Ant like blue bananas?   Yes, she does.
Does Bill like blue bananas?   Yes, he does.

Look

Does Annie like spaghetti?
Yes, she does.
She likes spaghetti and ice cream.

Does Bill like spaghetti and ice cream?
No, he doesn't.
He doesn't like spaghetti and ice cream.

Remember
doesn't = does not

16

Ask and answer

Does Pete like ice cream?

Yes, he does.
He likes chocolate ice cream.

- chocolate
- banana
- strawberry
- lemon

Play a game

Crocky Crocodile likes...

A Does Crocky like green lions?

B No, he doesn't.

A Does Crocky like red monkeys?

B Yes, he does.
   He likes red monkeys.

Delicious!

- blue frogs
- green lions
- red monkeys
- orange penguins

thirty-one 31

Lesson 17   Where does he come from?

Listen

Come here, children. Press V for visit.

We're off to a radio station.

Listen and point

This is Danny Banks on Radio Five.
This is Danny Banks on Radio Six.
Where do you come from?
Where does he come from?
I come from Scotland.
I come from Italy.
I've got two brothers and two sisters.
I've got two brothers and one sister.

He comes from... 17

Look

This is Pete's family.
His mother's name is Jane.
She comes from London.
His father's name is George.
He comes from New York.
His grandfather's name is Albert.
His grandmother's name is Poppy.
She comes from Greece.
Pete's got one brother, John.
He's got two sisters, Sally and Anna.

Ask each other

- What's your father's name?
- My father's name is...
- How many brothers and sisters have you got?

Say

Father, mother
Father, mother
What about me?

Sisters, brothers
Sisters, brothers
I can't see

Grandfather
And grandmother
Don't forget me!

Lesson 18   Does it...?   It doesn't ...

Listen

1. Guess the animal, Polly.
2. Is it big? / No, it isn't.
3. Does it bark? / No, it doesn't.
4. Does it like cats? / No, it doesn't. It hates cats.
5. Is it a mouse?
6. Yes, it is. Look!

Ask and answer

Does it bark?
Does it like cats?
Does it hate cats?
Is it big or small?

18

Look

It's a bird.
It hates cats.
It doesn't bark.

It's a cat.
It eats birds.
It doesn't like dogs.

Ask and answer

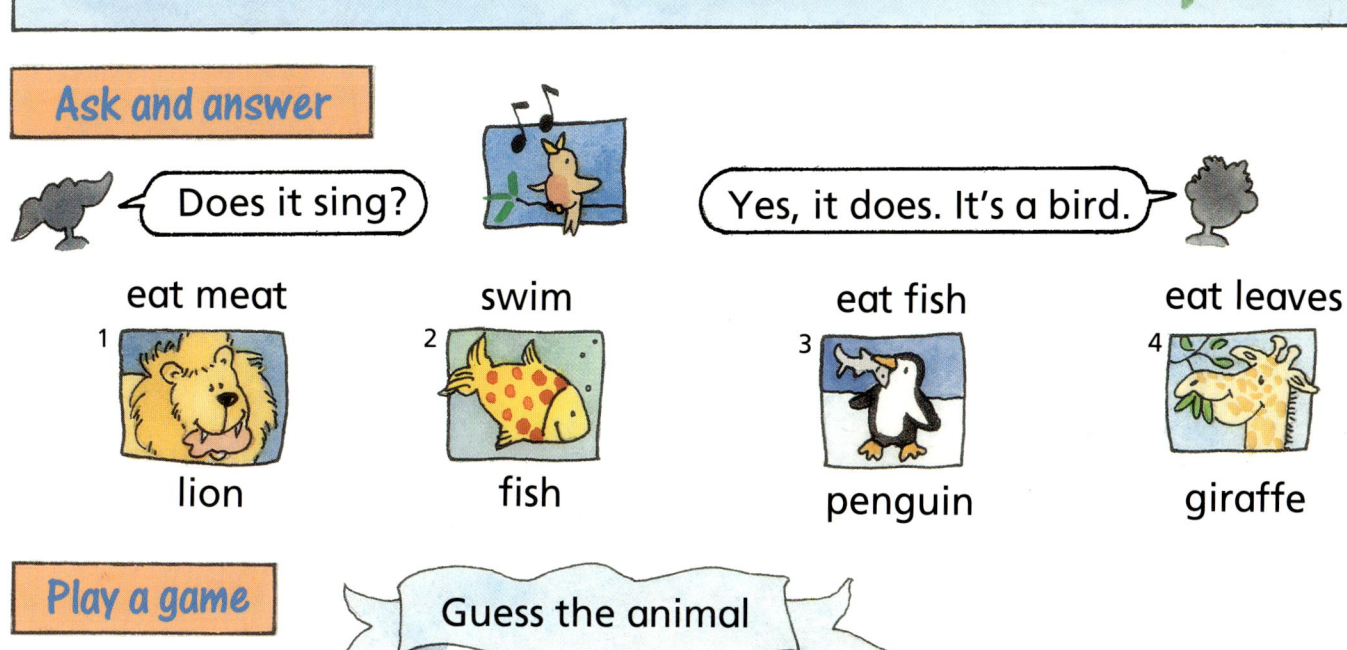

Does it sing?

Yes, it does. It's a bird.

1. eat meat — lion
2. swim — fish
3. eat fish — penguin
4. eat leaves — giraffe

Play a game

Guess the animal

Choose an animal: lion, giraffe, hippo, penguin, cat, mouse, frog, shark.

thirty-five 35

Lesson 19 Spring, Summer, Autumn, Winter

Look

Seasons of the year

Point and say

Snowflakes fall.
Flowers don't grow.

New leaves grow on trees.

It's summer.

It's autumn.

It's winter.

It's spring.

Leaves turn brown.
They fall.

Flowers grow.
Trees are green.

Ask and answer

Do flowers grow in summer?

Do leaves turn brown in spring?

Yes, they do.

No, they don't.

Do new leaves grow in autumn?
Do snowflakes fall in summer?
Do leaves turn brown in autumn?
Do flowers grow in winter?
Do new leaves grow in spring?

Look

It's hot. | It's cold. | It's windy. | It's raining.

Tell each other

- Take your umbrella.
- It's raining.

- Don't take your coat.
- It's hot.

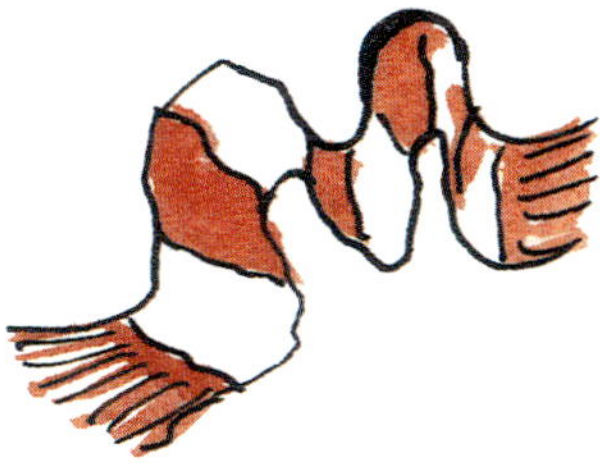

Listen

What are we?

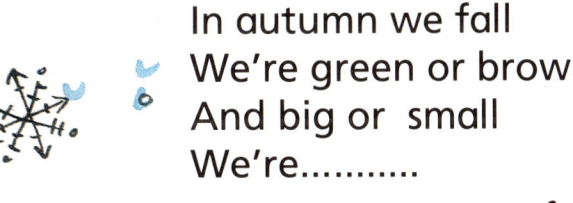

In spring we're new
In autumn we fall
We're green or brown
And big or small
We're..........

It's cold, we fall
But we're not old
We're new and white
We're..........

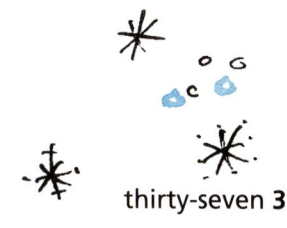

Lesson 20 How many...are there?

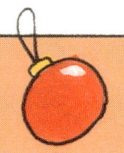

Look

December		April	
Sunday	3 10 17 24 31	Sunday	7 14 21 28
Monday	4 11 18 25	Monday	1 8 15 22 29
Tuesday	5 12 19 26	Tuesday	2 9 16 23 30
Wednesday	6 13 20 27	Wednesday	3 10 17 24
Thursday	7 14 21 28	Thursday	4 11 18 25
Friday	1 8 15 22 29	Friday	5 12 19 26
Saturday	2 9 16 23 30	Saturday	6 13 20 27

Ask and answer

 How many Sundays are there in April?   Four.

How many Mondays are there in December?
How many Thursdays are there in April?
How many Wednesdays are there in December?
How many Fridays are there in December?
How many Tuesdays are there in April?
How many Saturdays are there in December?
How many days are there in December?
How many days are there in April?

   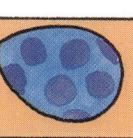 

20

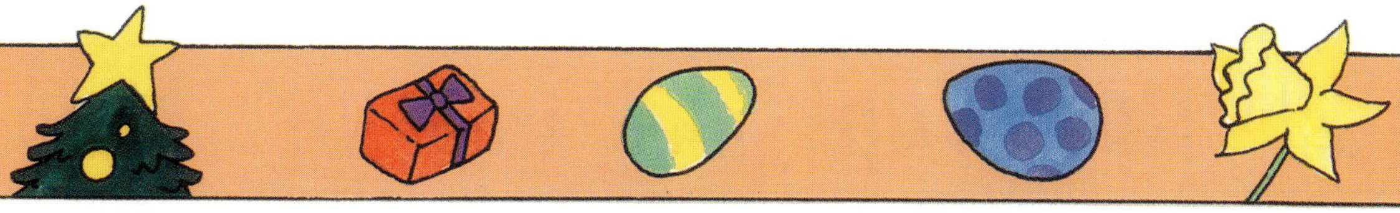

Read and decide

Say ' **Yes, that's right.** ' or ' **No, that's wrong.** '

There are five Sundays in December.
There are five Sundays in April.
There are four Fridays in December.
There are four Saturdays in April.
There are five Tuesdays in April.
There are four Wednesdays in December.

Ask and answer

What's this number? 37 — It's thirty-seven.
What's this number? 73 — It's seventy-three.

31 13 52 25 74 47 81 18

Play a game

Touch the squares

Close your eyes.
Touch two squares.
What's the number?

It's thirty-eight or eighty-three.

thirty-nine 39

Lesson 21 Speak up! pink tree

Listen and point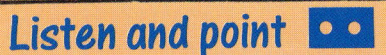

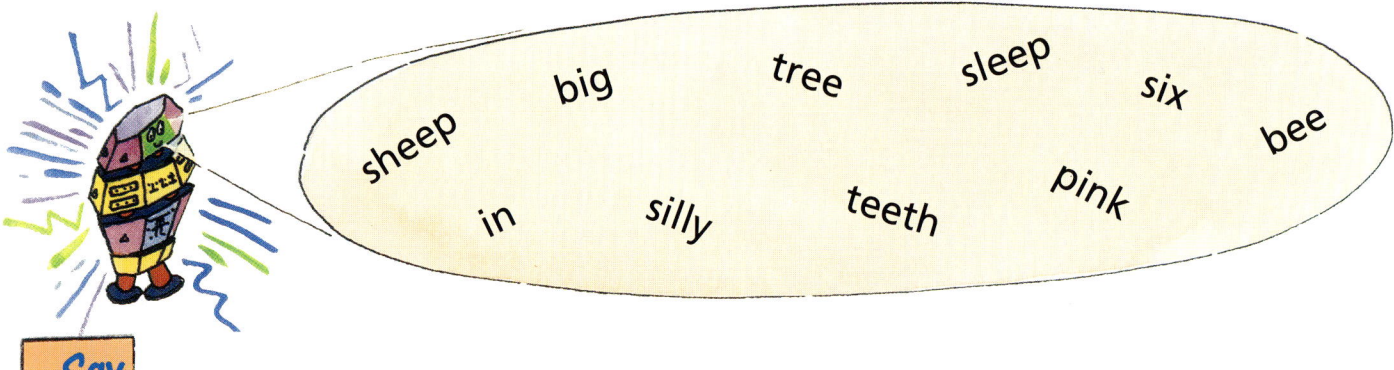

Say

1

2

3

4

Say

I can't sleep so I'm counting sheep
One, two, three, four
Big sheep, little sheep, more and more
I can't sleep so I'm counting sheep

I can't sleep so I'm counting teeth
One, two, three, four
Green teeth, pink teeth, more and more
I can't sleep so I'm counting teeth

I can't count any more I'm feeling sleepy...

Lesson 22   Revision 3

A Copy and complete

1 Do you like bananas?
   Yes, ...
2 Do you like blue bananas?
   No, ...
3 Does Annie like pink spaghetti?
   Yes, ...
4 Does Bill like pink spaghetti?
   No, ...
5 Where does he come from?
   He .... London.
6 Do flowers grow in summer?
   Yes, ...
7 Do leaves turn brown in summer?
   No, ...
8 Does Crocky .... green lions?
   No, ... He likes blue frogs.

C Copy and complete

1 ....?
   She comes from London.
2 .... brothers and sisters.........?
   I've got one brother and one sister.

D Complete these words

1 m _ t h _ r
2 g _ _ n d m _ t _ e _
3 f _ _ h _ r
4 g r _ _ _ f a _ _ _ r
5 s _ s _ e _

E Write

I like....... / I don't like.......

B Say

Now I can:
- talk about things I like.
- talk about my family.
- talk about animals.
- talk about the seasons.
- talk about the weather.

Put your **Bravo!** sticker here

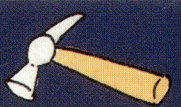

Look

Is she making a house?
No, she isn't.

Is he flying a kite?
Yes, he is.

Ask and answer

 Is she eating an ice cream?

1

Yes, she is.

painting a picture

flying a kite

reading a book

singing a song

playing on a computer

2

3

4

5

6

Lesson 24 What is it?

Listen

1. What is it, Annie?
   Look. Look inside.
2. It's very nice.
   What are you doing? Get out!
3. Good night, Annie.
   It isn't a bed.
4. It's very comfortable.
   Wake up, wake up.

Listen and match

The box is	the box.
Annie isn't	Bill's bed.
Bill and Andy Ant like	happy.
It isn't	Andy's bed.
It isn't	comfortable.

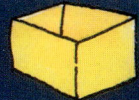  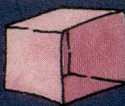 

24

Look

Are Bill and Andy Ant sleeping?
Yes, they are.

Are Bill and Andy Ant flying a kite?
No, they aren't.

Ask and answer

Are they playing football or volleyball?

They're playing volleyball.

reading a book or watching TV?   juggling or running?   playing the piano or painting?

Play a game

Choose a sentence.

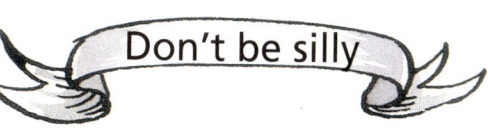

I'm eating an umbrella.   I'm sitting on a kite.   I'm flying a car.

I'm reading an elephant.

Don't be silly! You aren't reading an elephant. You're reading a book.

forty-five 45

Lesson 25 Can I try your...?

Listen

Come here please, children.
Press V for visit.

We're off to an ice cream factory.

Listen and point

We are looking at the milk for the ice cream.
We are looking at the ice cream.

Our ice cream hasn't got milk in it.
Our ice cream has got milk in it.

Do you like ice cream?
Does he like ice cream?

Can we try the ice cream?
Can we eat the ice cream?

25

Look

Can I try your ice cream?
Yes, you can.
Can I try your hat?
No, you can't.

Ask and answer

Can I try your...?

1
2
3
4
5
6
7

Say

Do you like ice cream, ice cream, ice cream?
Do you like ice cream?
Yes, I do

Does he like ice cream, ice cream, ice cream?
Does he like ice cream?
Yes, he does

Do we like ice cream, ice cream, ice cream?
Do we like ice cream?
Yes, we do

Ice cream, ice cream
Delicious ice cream

But I don't like ice cream.

Lesson 26 I don't know

Listen

1. What's the code for Electrobox?
   I don't know. I haven't got my keypad.
2. Let's try YZARC.
3. Is YZARC a word?
   No, it isn't. It's a secret code.
4. This code is wrong.
   Oh, dear! Electrobox is hot.
5. Very hot. What are you doing? Press 'STOP'.
6.
7. Are you CRAZY?

Ask and answer

1. Has Pete got his keypad?
2. Is YZARC a secret code?
3. Is the code right?
4. Is Electrobox hot?
5. Is Miss Electra happy?

26

Look

Ask and answer

Play a game

Crazy animals

Choose an animal.
A The monkey has got the penguin's head.
B The penguin has got the lion's head.

Lesson 27 It's cloudy

Look

It's raining.   It's sunny.   It's windy.
It's snowing.   It's cloudy.   It's foggy.

Point and say

It's sunny.   Let's go to the beach.

go to the beach

jump in puddles

play on the computer

play football

make a snowman

fly a kite

50 fifty

Lesson 28   breakfast   lunch   dinner

Look

Polly gets up at seven o' clock.
She has breakfast at eight o' clock.
She has lunch at half past one.
She has dinner at half past eight.
She goes to bed at half past nine.

Read and decide

Say 'Yes, that's right.' or 'No, that's wrong.'

Mr and Mrs Spooky get up at six o' clock.
They have breakfast at half past seven.
They have lunch at half past twelve.
They have dinner at nine o' clock.
They go to bed at eleven o' clock.

Ask each other

What time do you get up?   I get up at...

28

Number game

How many sandwiches do the monsters eat in one day?

I'm the green monster. I'm the blue monster.

1. Start here
2. You're having 3 sandwiches for breakfast.
3. You're running. Go foward 1
4. 4 Sandwiches
5. You're having 10 sandwiches for lunch.
6. 3 sandwiches
7. You're sleeping. Go back 1
8. 5 sandwiches
9. 2 sandwiches
10. You're juggling. Go back 1
11. You're playing football. Go foward 1
12. 6 Sandwiches
13. 8 sandwiches
14. You're having 2 sandwiches for dinner.
15. You're washing. Go back 4
16. 3 Sandwiches
17. 9 Sandwiches
18. You're watching T.V. Go back 3
19. 12 Sandwiches
20. You're going to bed. How many sandwiches?

FINISH

fifty-three 53

Lesson 29 Speak up! taxi bus

Listen and point

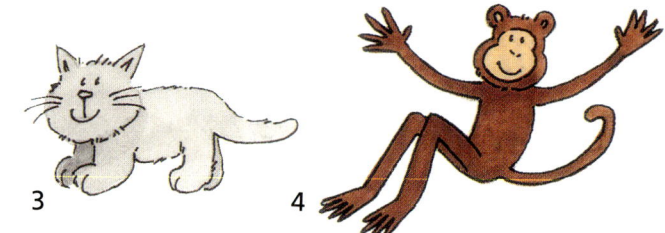

Say

1 2 3 4

Sing ♪

It's a sunny summer's day
Can we pack our bags and go?
It's fun, it's fun, on a summer's day
To pack our bags and go

It's a sunny summer's day
Can we catch a bus and go?
It's fun, it's fun, on a summer's day
To catch a bus and go

It's a sunny summer's day
Can we have our lunch and go?
It's fun, it's fun, on a summer's day
To have our lunch and go

Yes, you can!

54 fifty-four

Lesson 30 Revision 4

A Copy and complete

1 Is she making a box?
   Yes, ...
2 Is he making a kite?
   No, ...
3 Are they juggling?
   No, ...
4 What .... doing?
   I'm reading a book.
5 .... are .... doing?
   I'm eating a pizza.
6 Can I try your bike?
   No, ...
7 Can I try your ice cream?
   Yes, ...
8 Can I try your chips?
   No, ...
9 What's this?
   I .... know.
10 What colour are your socks?
   They're ....

B Say

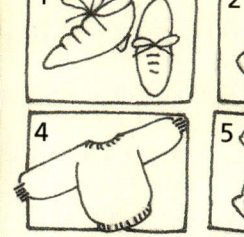
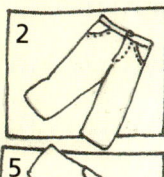
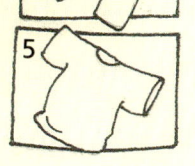
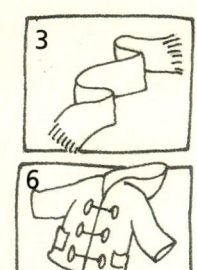

C Copy and complete

1 .... doing?
   They're playing tennis.
2 .... try.......... pen?
   Yes, you can.
3 What ....your shirt?
   It's blue.
4 What .... are your shoes?
   They're brown.

D Copy and complete

1 .... penguin's head.
2 .... giraffe's..........
3 ....dog's ....

Now I can:
■ ask 'What are you doing?'
■ use 'Can I...?'
■ Talk about meals.
■ use 'I don't know'.
■ talk about clothes.

Lesson 31   I'm going to be a...

Listen

1. — Hello, Bill. I've got an idea.
   — What is it, Annie?

2. — I'm going to grow spaghetti. Look, spaghetti trees. I'm going to be a millionaire.

3. — You aren't going to be a millionaire. Spaghetti doesn't grow on trees.
   — Oh, dear. Never mind.

4. — I've got another idea. Let's eat spaghetti.
   — Yes, let's. That's a good idea.

5.

56 fifty-six

31

Look

Ask each other

1 bus driver
2 computer expert
3 scientist
4 explorer
5 nurse
6 astronaut
7 doctor
8 teacher
9 football player

Play a game

A Are you going to be an astronaut?

B No, I'm not. I'm going to be a...

fifty-seven 57

Lesson 32 on the left   on the right

Listen

Come here please, children.
Press V for visit.

We're off to an airport.

Listen and match

We're going to look inside   big aeroplane?
The passenger lounge is   an aeroplane.
Today we're visiting   on the left.
Can you see the   an airport.

 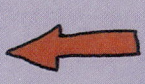  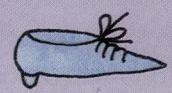 

32

Look

The toys are on the left.　　　　　　　The books are on the right.

Ask and answer

Where are the apples?　　They're on the right.

Say

Hurry up, hurry up, we're going to be late
Hurry up, hurry up, I just can't wait

Where's my shoe and where's my hat?
Where's my sock and where's the cat?

Where are my tickets and where are my keys?
Where are my gloves and where are my skis?

fifty-nine 59

Lesson 33 Where's Electrobox?

Listen

1. Come inside. We're going to take off.
   Electrobox isn't an aeroplane!

2. Come inside. Hurry up, hurry up. We're going to take off.

3.

4. Where's Miss Electra?
   Where's Electrobox?

5. Do you know?

33

Read and decide

Say ' Yes, that's right.' , ' No, that's wrong.' or ' I don't know.'

Miss Electra is in Electrobox.
Polly is in Electrobox.
Pete isn't in Electrobox.
Electrobox is going to take off.
Miss Electra is crazy.
The children are happy.
Max is in Electrobox.

Ask each other

What are we going to do?

Where's Miss Electra?

Come on, Rover. Where's Electrobox?

I don't know.

Lesson 34 Revision 5

A Copy and complete

1. Is Annie going to be a millionaire?
   No, ...
2. Are you going to be an astronaut?
   No, ...
3. Is he going to be a scientist?
   Yes, ...
4. I'm going to eat lots of spaghetti.
   That's ....idea.
5. I'm going to wash the cat.
   Don't ....silly!

5. Where are the rubbers?
   ....right.
6. Where are the pencils?
   .... left.

C Say

B Copy and complete

1. Where's the pen?
   .... the book.
2. Where's the pencil sharpener?
   .... the rulers.
3. Where are the rulers?
   .... the book.
4. Where's the box?
   ....the chair.

Now I can:
- ☐ use 'going to'.
- ☐ talk about 'right' and 'left'.
- ☐ use 'That's a good idea'.

Put your Bravo! sticker here

My dictionary

Animals
bee
bird
giraffe
hippo
lion
monkey
penguin
shark

Days of the week
Monday
Tuesday
Wednesday
Thursday
Friday
Saturday
Sunday

Family
brother
sister
mother
father
grandfather
grandmother

Food
bananas
chicken
chips
chocolate
grapes
meat
milk
peaches
pears
sandwich
strawberry
vanilla

Jobs
astronaut
bus driver
computer expert
doctor
explorer
nurse
scientist

Months of the year
January
February
March
April
May
June
July
August
September
October
November
December

Weather
cloudy
cold
foggy
hot
raining
snowing
sunny
windy

Heinemann International
A division of Heinemann Publishers (Oxford) Ltd
Halley Court, Jordan Hill, Oxford, OX2 8EJ

OXFORD LONDON EDINBURGH
MADRID ATHENS BOLOGNA PARIS
MELBOURNE SYDNEY AUCKLAND SINGAPORE TOKYO
IBADAN NAIROBI HARARE GABORONE
PORTSMOUTH (NH)

ISBN 0 435 29195 5

© Judy West   C.J. Moore   1993

All rights reserved; no part of this publication may be reproduced, stored in a retrieval system, or transmitted in any form or by any means, electronic, mechanical, photocopying, recording, or otherwise, without the prior written permission of the Publishers.

First published 1993

Designed by Ranjit Rai-Quantrill

Illustrated by Rebecca Archer, Lorraine White and Jaqueline East

Acknowledgements
The author and publishers would like to thank the following for permission to reproduce copyright photographs: Robert Estall Photographs p46 and
Chris Allan Aviation Library p58. Thanks also to B.B.C. Radio Oxford,
Caterskill Management Limited and Temple Cowley Middle School, Oxford.
Commissioned photography by Sue Baker
Picture Research by Mandy Twells

The authors would like to thank Kate Melliss, Amanda Cant and
Ranjit Rai-Quantrill for their help in the preparation and design of this book.

Printed and bound in Hong Kong

93 94 95 96 97 10 9 8 7 6 5 4 3 2 1